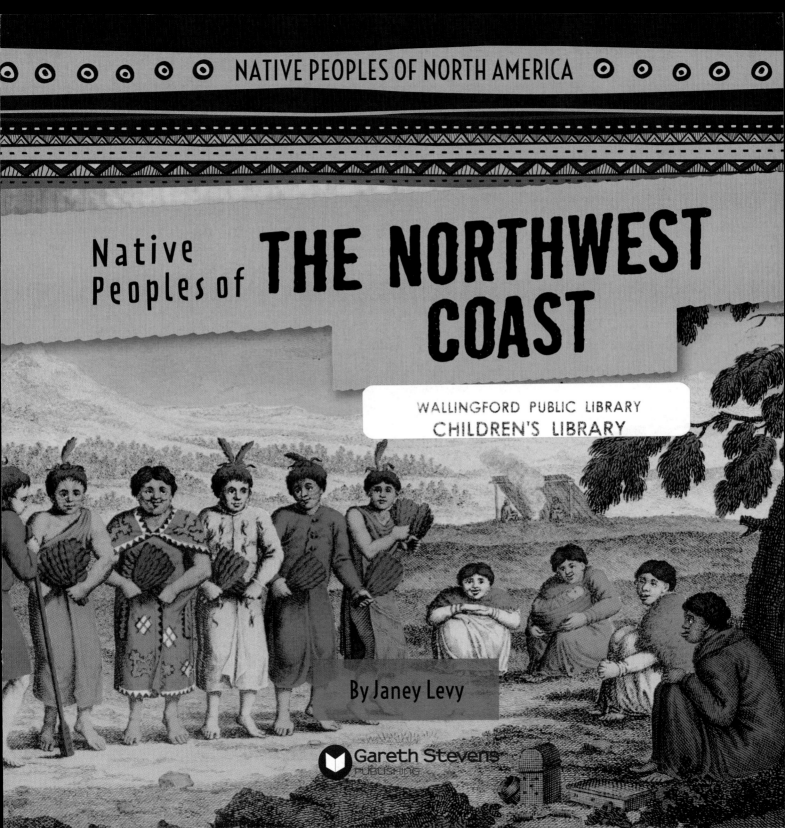

Native Peoples of THE NORTHWEST COAST

By Janey Levy

Gareth Stevens
PUBLISHING

Please visit our website, www.garethstevens.com. For a free color catalog of all our high-quality books, call toll free 1-800-542-2595 or fax 1-877-542-2596.

Library of Congress Cataloging-in-Publication Data

Names: Levy, Janey, author.
Title: Native peoples of the Northwest coast / Janey Levy.
Description: New York : Gareth Stevens Publishing, 2017. | Series: Native
  peoples of North America | Includes index.
Identifiers: LCCN 2015050139 | ISBN 9781482448276 (pbk.) | ISBN 9781482448160 (library bound) | ISBN
9781482447637 (6 pack)
Subjects: LCSH: Indians of North America–Northwest Coast of North
  America–History–Juvenile literature.
Classification: LCC E78.N78 L48 2017 | DDC 978.004/97–dc23
LC record available at http://lccn.loc.gov/2015050139

First Edition

Published in 2017 by
Gareth Stevens Publishing
111 East 14th Street, Suite 349
New York, NY 10003

Copyright © 2017 Gareth Stevens Publishing

Designer: Samantha DeMartin
Editor: Kristen Nelson

Photo credits: Series art AlexTanya/Shutterstock.com; cover, p. 1 Three Lions/Hulton Archive/Getty Images; p. 5 (main) Jarred Decker/Shutterstock.com; p. 5 (map) AlexCovarrubias/Wikimedia Commons; pp. 7, 13 Werner Forman/Universal Images Group/Getty Images; p. 9 (both) courtesy of the Library of Congress; pp. 11, 17 (left inset) Wolfgang Kaehler/LightRocket/Getty Images; pp. 15, 19 Marilyn Angel Wynn/Nativestock/Getty Images; p. 17 (right inset) Chris Cheadle/All Canada Photos/Getty Images; p. 17 (main) oksana.perkins/Shutterstock.com; p. 21 Rebecca E. Marvil/Photolibrary/Getty Images; p. 23 Jeff Schultz/Design Pics/First Light/Getty Images; p. 25 (main) Bill Peters/Denver Post/Getty Images; p. 25 (inset) courtesy of The Metropolitan Museum of Art; p. 27 akphotoc/Shutterstock.com.

Printed in the United States of America

CPSIA compliance information: Batch #CS16GS. For further information contact Gareth Stevens, New York, New York at 1-800-542-2595.

CONTENTS

Words in the glossary appear in **bold** type the first time they are used in the text.

North America's
NORTHWEST COAST

The Northwest Coast runs along North America's Pacific shore from Alaska to northern California. Along the way, it passes through British Columbia in Canada and the US states of Washington and Oregon.

The land rises steeply from the coast to form mountains covered by cedar and spruce forests. Because it's so far north, the area never gets too hot. And a Pacific Ocean current brings warm air, so it never gets too cold. The favorable conditions drew the first people there around 11,000 years ago.

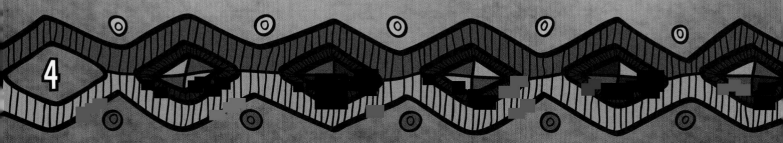

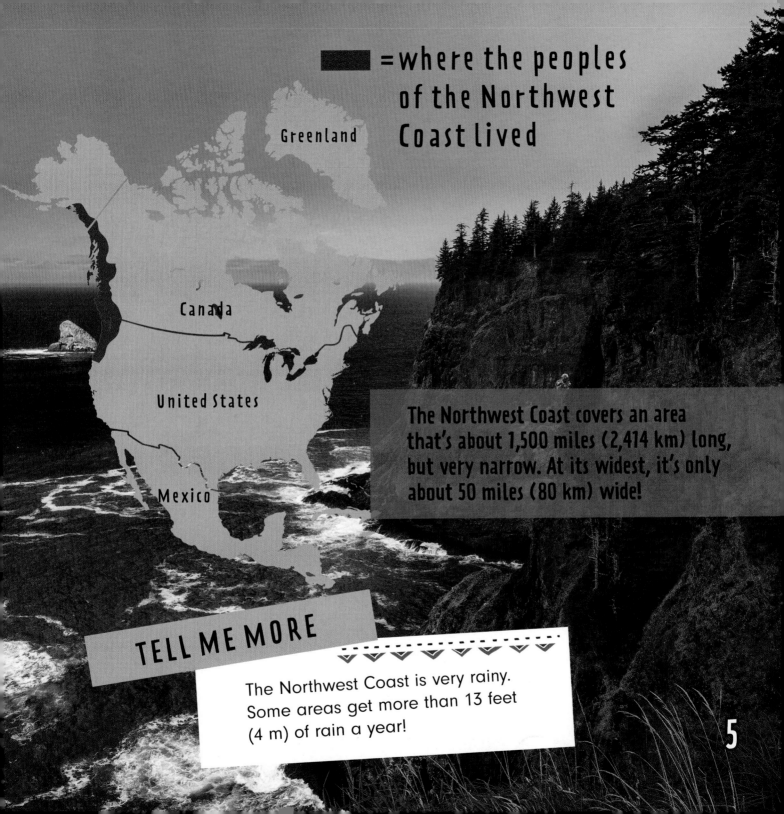

= where the peoples of the Northwest Coast lived

Greenland

Canada

United States

Mexico

The Northwest Coast covers an area that's about 1,500 miles (2,414 km) long, but very narrow. At its widest, it's only about 50 miles (80 km) wide!

TELL ME MORE

The Northwest Coast is very rainy. Some areas get more than 13 feet (4 m) of rain a year!

5

Fishing, Gathering, and Trading
SOCIETIES

The **ancestors** of the Northwest Coast native peoples found a place rich in **natural resources**. Over time, they created more than 50 societies that shared many common features.

Northwest Coast peoples fished and caught ocean **mammals** such as whales, seals, and sea otters. From the forests, they gathered wild plants and sometimes hunted animals such as deer and moose. They also traded with each other and with peoples far away. In this way, they brought new goods to their community and improved their life.

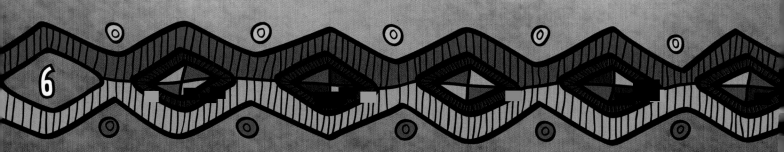

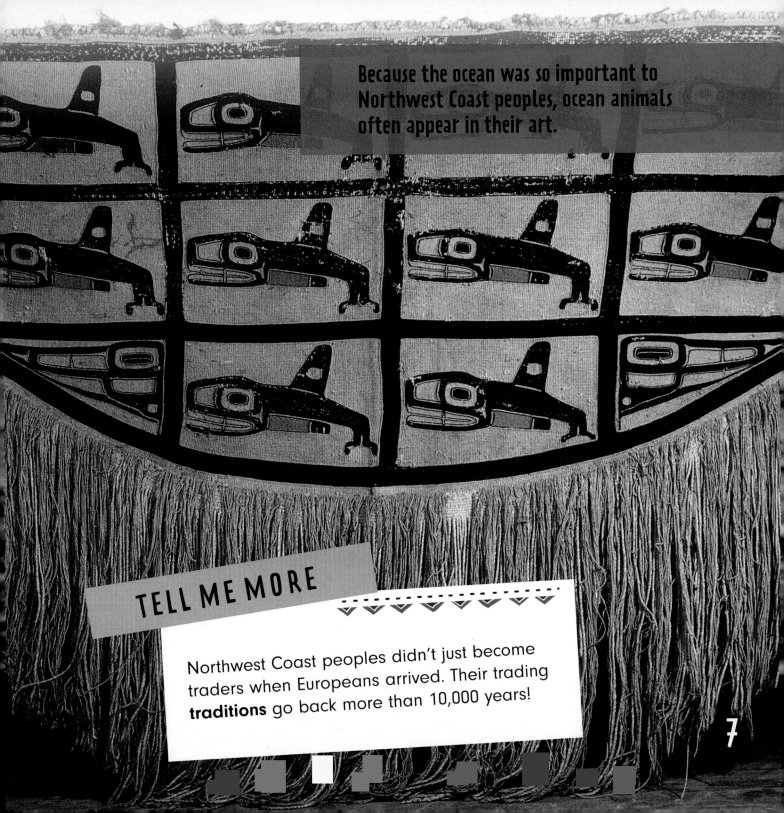

Because the ocean was so important to Northwest Coast peoples, ocean animals often appear in their art.

TELL ME MORE

Northwest Coast peoples didn't just become traders when Europeans arrived. Their trading **traditions** go back more than 10,000 years!

7

Men's Jobs, Women's JOBS

Among Northwest Coast native peoples, some jobs were for men, some were for women, and some were for both. Men fished and hunted, went to war when necessary, and could serve as chief. Women gathered plants and did most of the childcare and cooking. Men and women both took part in storytelling, making art and music, and the work of healing.

There was, however, one way women could be leaders. Northwest Coast societies had a **clan** system. And women could be clan leaders.

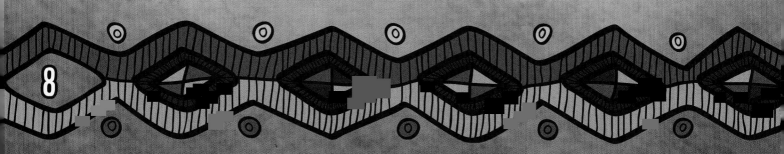

8

Northwest Coast societies had social classes. The woman shown here was a chief's daughter, and her clothing shows her importance. Her earrings and the decorations on her hat were made from the shell of a sea animal that only high-ranking people were allowed to use.

TELL ME MORE

Children always belonged to their mother's clan.

Villages and HOMES

For Northwest Coast peoples, their main home was in their winter village. Villages were located on the Pacific coast or along the shore of a river or lake. During warm weather, the people separated into small groups and moved to places to fish or gather berries. When winter returned, they went back to their winter village.

Their homes were large rectangular buildings made of cedar planks, or boards. Several families from the same clan lived in each house.

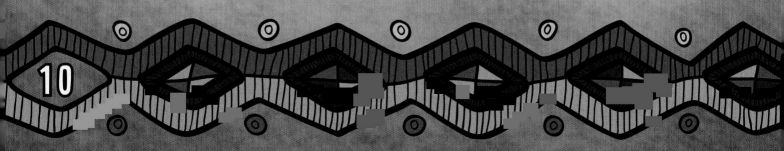

The front of the house was commonly painted with pictures of **mythical** beings.

TELL ME MORE

The planks of the houses were fixed to a sturdy **permanent** frame. They could be taken off and carried along as the people moved from place to place.

11

The Spirit WORLD

Northwest Coast peoples believed a spirit world surrounded them. This included a **guardian spirit** for each person. The guardian spirit gave the person a basic skill, such as making baskets, fishing, or, in special cases, the knowledge to be a shaman.

Salmon, which were an important food for Northwest Coast peoples, were considered magical beings. Once a year, they became fish and swam up streams so people could catch them. If people treated them with respect, they would return year after year.

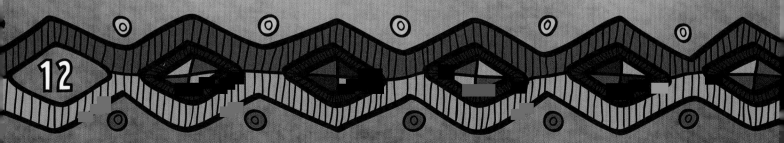

A shaman was a man or woman who could speak with the spirit world and had the ability to both heal and harm people.

Because of salmon's importance, they appeared in the art of Northwest Coast peoples, such as this rattle.

13

The Potlatch
CEREMONY

The potlatch **ceremony** was a special feature of Northwest Coast societies. The word "potlatch" comes from a trading term used throughout the area and means "to give." Potlatches were held to mark events of social importance such as weddings, births, deaths, or the building of a house.

A potlatch might last 3 weeks and included feasting, singing, and dancing. Most importantly, it included giving gifts to the guests. The more wealth a family gave away, the more honor it received.

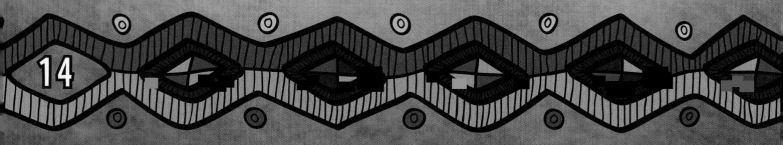

The potlatch was banned by the Canadian government from 1884 to 1951, but is now practiced again.

TELL ME MORE

It could take years to plan and prepare for a potlatch.

Totem Poles and Ceremonial MASKS

Northwest Coast peoples are famous for their totem poles and ceremonial masks. The towering totem poles were carved, or cut, from cedar trees. They featured both human and animal forms. Several types existed. Some stood against the house front and often served as the door. Some were inside the house and held up the roof. Others stood alone to honor dead chiefs.

Carved and painted wooden masks were an important part of all ceremonies, including the potlatch. Copper masks were a sign of wealth.

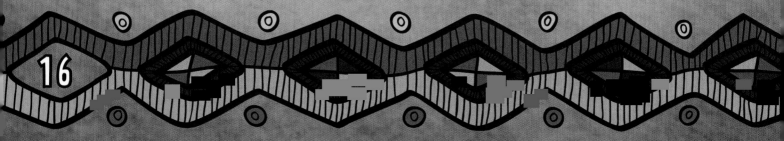

This totem pole can be seen in the Totem Bight State Historical Park in Ketchikan, Alaska.

TELL ME MORE

Totem poles were usually painted black, red, and blue, sometimes with white and yellow.

17

The Tlingit, or the "PEOPLE"

The Tlingit are one of the most well-known Northwest Coast peoples. Their name comes from the word they called themselves, which means "people."

The Tlingit were famous for their Chilkat blankets, which were so highly prized that only the wealthy could afford to make or own them. The blankets were made from mountain goat wool and cedar bark. Men created the pattern and supplied the goat hides for the wool. Women gathered the cedar bark, prepared the yarn, and made the blanket.

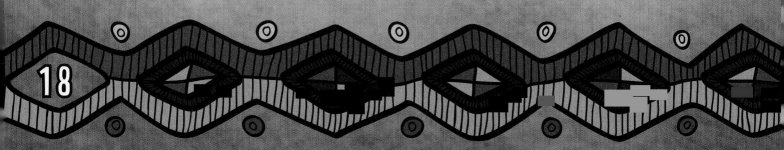

Chilkat blankets were and still are worn by dancers on special occasions.

TELL ME MORE

It took as long as a year to make a Chilkat blanket.

The People from
HAIDA GWAII

Another well-known people of the Northwest Coast is the Haida. Their ancient tales say they came to modern-day southeastern Alaska long ago from islands called Haida Gwaii. The islands had come to be called the Queen Charlotte Islands, but in 2010 they were officially renamed Haida Gwaii to honor the history of the Haida Nation.

The Haida's special claim to fame was their skill in crafting **dugout canoes**. All Northwest Coast peoples made dugout canoes, but the Haida were considered the most skilled canoe makers.

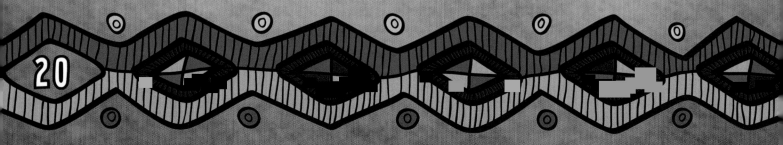

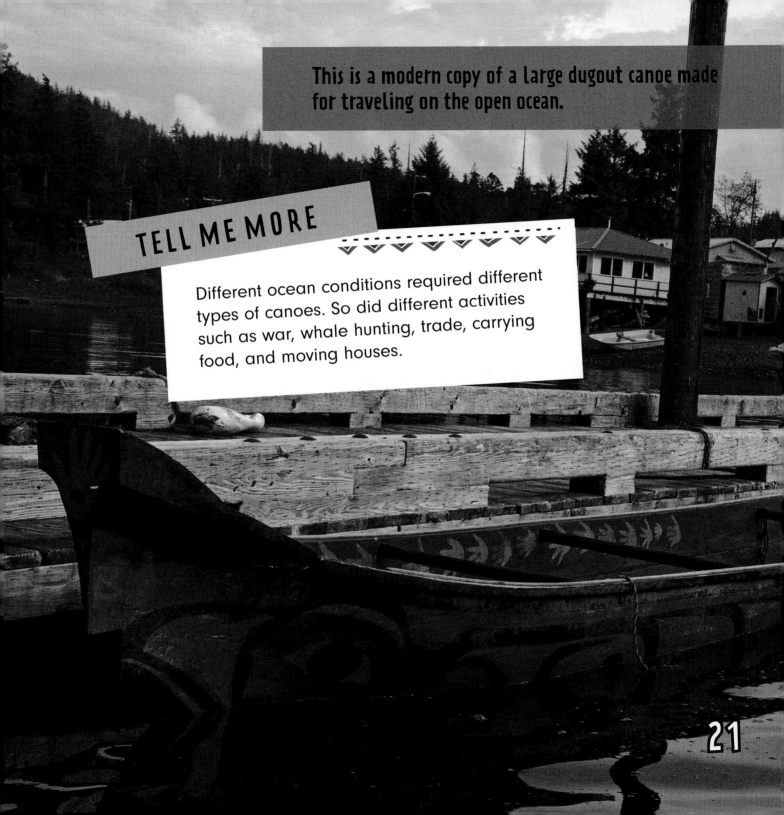

This is a modern copy of a large dugout canoe made for traveling on the open ocean.

TELL ME MORE

Different ocean conditions required different types of canoes. So did different activities such as war, whale hunting, trade, carrying food, and moving houses.

The People Inside the
SKEENA RIVER

The Tsimshian people are also well-known. Their name means "people inside the Skeena River." It comes from the fact that they lived along the Skeena and the Nass Rivers in what's now British Columbia, Canada.

The Tsimshian people gained wealth from their control of the candlefish oil trade. The women had a special method for getting the **nutritious** oil out of the fish. It included letting the fish rot for up to 3 weeks and then boiling the rotten fish!

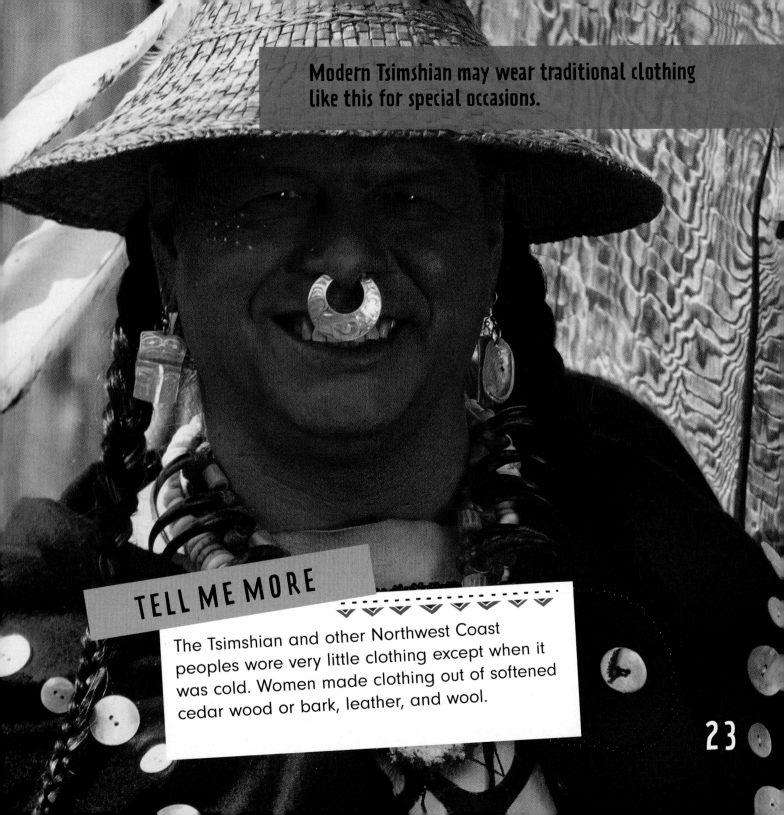

Modern Tsimshian may wear traditional clothing like this for special occasions.

TELL ME MORE

The Tsimshian and other Northwest Coast peoples wore very little clothing except when it was cold. Women made clothing out of softened cedar wood or bark, leather, and wool.

23

Speakers of the Kwak'wala
LANGUAGE

Along the coast of British Columbia and Vancouver Island lived native people who spoke a language called Kwak'wala. They're often called Kwakiutl today, but they call themselves Kwakwaka'wakw, which means "speakers of the Kwak'wala language."

Their society was ordered by rank, which was based largely on rights a person received from their parents. Many of these rights had to do with Kwakwaka'wakw ceremonies, which were an important part of life. The rights may have included the right to sing certain songs and wear certain masks.

Masks became even more special as they were passed down in families over many years.

TELL ME MORE

The Kwakwaka'wakw are perhaps the most well-known of all Northwest Coast peoples, although nonnatives are likely most familiar with the name "Kwakiutl."

25

The Coast Salish-Speaking PEOPLES

The term "Coast Salish" has to do with a language family and is applied to the Northwest Coast peoples who spoke those languages. Coast Salish peoples lived in modern-day southwestern British Columbia in Canada and the US state of Washington for about 11,000 years.

Like other Northwest Coast peoples, the Coast Salish showed respect for what the earth supplied through First Foods ceremonies. These honored traditional foods and were held, for example, when the first salmon were caught or first berries were picked.

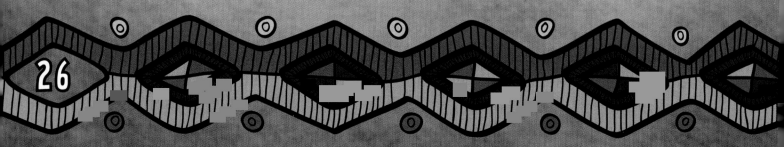

The Coast Salish used totem poles to honor their ancestors and the spirit world.

TELL ME MORE

The Coast Salish called the western red cedar the "tree of life" because it supplied the basic matter to make canoes, houses, clothing, tools, and baskets.

Northwest Coast Native Peoples TODAY

Contact with Europeans in the late 1700s brought hard times for Northwest Coast peoples. Illnesses the Europeans brought killed large numbers of native peoples. Europeans took over native lands. Native children were forced to attend schools far away and give up their traditions and language.

Today, things look better. The population of Northwest Coast peoples has grown to over 100,000. Ceremonies like the potlatch are experiencing a rebirth. And Northwest Coast peoples are forcing governments to recognize their rights to their land and their ways of life.

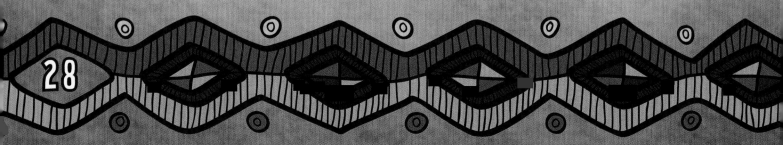

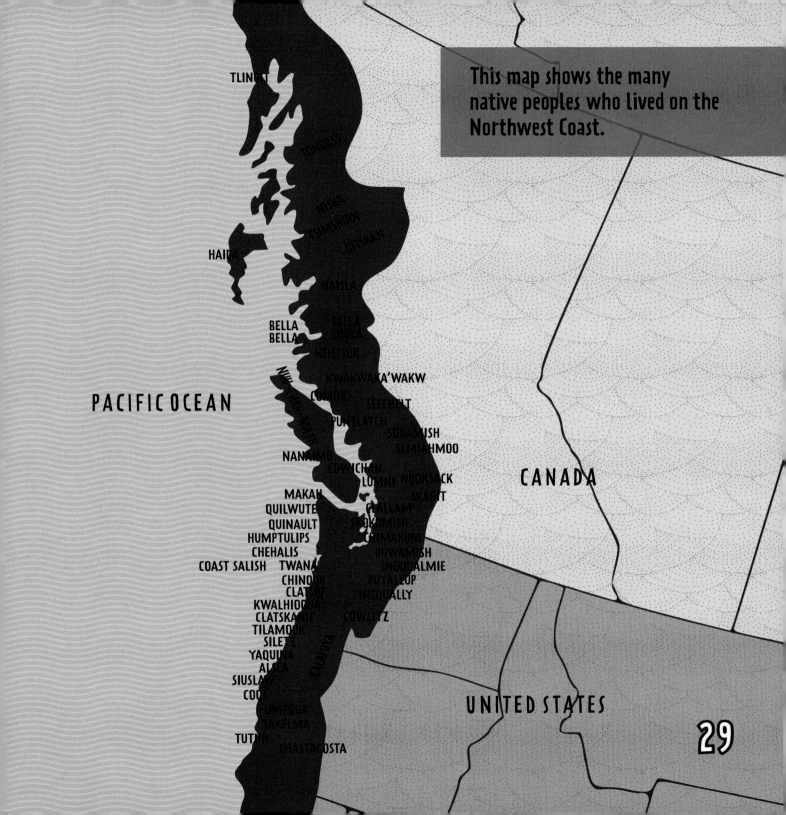

This map shows the many native peoples who lived on the Northwest Coast.

PACIFIC OCEAN

CANADA

UNITED STATES

TLINGIT
TONGASS
NISKA
TSIMSHIAN
GITSKAN
HAIDA
HAISLA
BELLA COOLA
BELLA BELLA
HEILTSUK
KWAKWAKA'WAKW
NUU-CHAH-NULTH
COMOX
SEECHELT
PUNTLATCH
SQUAMISH
SEMIAHMOO
NANAIMO
COWICHAN
LUMMI
NOOKSACK
MAKAH
SKAGIT
QUILWUTE
CLALLAM
QUINAULT
SKOKOMISH
HUMPTULIPS
CHIMAKUM
CHEHALIS
DUWAMISH
COAST SALISH
TWANA
SNOQUALMIE
CHINOOK
PUYALLUP
CLATSOP
NISQUALLY
KWALHIOQUA
CLATSKANIE
COWLITZ
TILAMOOK
SILETZ
YAQUINA
KALAPUYA
ALSEA
SIUSLAW
COOS
UMPQUA
TAKELMA
TUTINI
CHASTACOSTA

29

GLOSSARY

ancestor: someone in your family who lived long before you

ceremony: an event to honor something

clan: a group of connected families

dugout canoe: a long, narrow boat made by hollowing out a large log

guardian spirit: a spirit believed to have special care for a certain person

mammal: a warm-blooded animal that has a backbone and hair, breathes air, and feeds milk to its young

mythical: like a story or tale

natural resource: something in nature that can be used by people

nutritious: having things needed to grow and stay alive

permanent: lasting

tradition: a long-practiced way of life

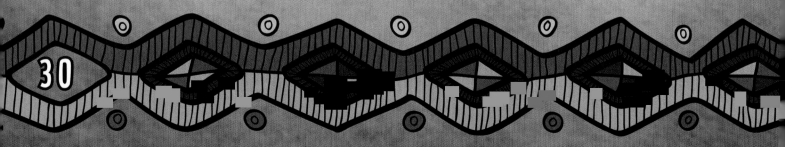

For More INFORMATION

Books

Simpson, Caroll. *The First Beaver*. Custer, WA: Heritage House, 2008.

Sonneborn, Liz. *Northwest Coast Indians*. Chicago, IL: Heinemann Library, 2012.

Websites

Hall of Northwest Coast Indians

www.amnh.org/exhibitions/permanent-exhibitions/human-origins-and-cultural-halls/hall-of-northwest-coast-indians

Take a tour of the hall and learn about Northwest Coast native peoples through the works they created.

Northwest Coastal People

firstpeoplesofcanada.com/fp_groups/fp_nwc5.html

This site uses pictures and text to dig into the stories of many of the native peoples of Canada's Northwest Coast.

INDEX